NOW
I HAVE SEEN
You

Kathi L. Norris et al.

ISBN 978-1-0980-8398-4 (paperback)
ISBN 978-1-0980-8399-1 (digital)

Christian Faith Publishing, Inc.
832 Park Avenue
Meadville, PA 16335
www.christianfaithpublishing.com

Photo credit for cover photo
- Sara Engel Photography

Printed in the United States of America

To our parents.
We see you still grieving today over the
great loss of Ted and Suzanne.
We miss them, and we know you miss them as well.
Their brothers and sisters miss them.
Their children and grandchildren miss them.

The world misses them too. It will never
realize how much it missed.

We love you deeply.

Elmer and Gloria Little
Wayne and Harriet Studebaker
Gary and Regie Buckmaster
Richard and Suzanne Norris
Perry and Marcelle Hack

I had only heard about you before, but
now I have seen you with my own eyes.
—Job 42:5 (NLT)

Contents

Foreword

Leigh and I have known Kathi for decades. She is the real deal. She is multitalented. She anticipates needs before they happen and finds ways to meet those needs. This book is evidence of that. Kathi's testimony is powerful. Kathi, thanks for collecting these stories. Kathi, thanks for sharing your own story. Also, thanks to everyone who shared your story. Read this book and allow the testimonies of courageous followers of Jesus provide you with stories of endurance and encouragement that will give you strength during your "dark night of the soul."

Dr. G. Steve and Leigh Kinnard
Teacher and Women's Ministry Leader
at New York City Church of Christ

Introduction

Now I Have Seen You

The heart of this book was born when my husband, who was only twenty-eight years old, died. I was a Christian and had searched high and low for two years looking through the scriptures for answers and direction during his illness. There were endless tears and crying out to God.

I remember reading the book of Job and thinking, *No one wants to be the person reading this book because you think you relate.* At the end of the book, chapter 42, Job says to God, "I had only heard about you before, but now I have seen you with my own eyes." I was so impacted! I realized that during the two years that my husband had been ill, I was able to see, with my own eyes, the *character of God* in a way that I never would have been able to otherwise.

Now, although I feel deeply for people going through incredibly tough times, I know they have the blessing of seeing God, and who he really is, in a way that they otherwise may have never seen. That is the heart of this book. As we see the character of God with our own eyes, we will then have the faith to move forward with our lives and rebuild.

In this book, my friends and family will share their stories with you. They are not professional writers. They aren't all written in the same narrative. They aren't all written in the same format. They don't all have happy endings. I choose to leave it that way, because each person is unique. Each story is special. Each one reaches out and says, "If I hadn't gone through this, I wouldn't have known God this well and *that* keeps me faithful!"

My prayer is that you will not only hear about God, but that you will see God in your life and that you will forever be faithful to him as well.

Grief—/grēf/

noun

1. Deep sorrow, especially that caused by someone's death
2. Keen mental suffering or distress over affliction or loss; sharp sorrow; painful regret
3. A cause or occasion of keen distress or sorrow

If you are reading this, I am assuming you fall into at least one of the following categories.

1. You are experiencing a recent and deep loss. It might not be a physical death as grief is involved to a greater or lesser degree in any loss.
2. Your loss is not recent but remains as painful as it was the day you first learned of their death. And you are seeking some inspiration in how to begin moving forward. I deliberately use the word *forward* as opposed to *moving on* which implies leaving something behind. You will never leave your loss behind. But you can and will learn to make space in your heart for the loss. By so doing, you can find peace.
3. You are a friend seeking guidance in how to help someone grappling with a serious loss.

I first want to offer my condolences. Loss sucks. It just does. I know as you do that death is a part of life. Yes, God can and does miraculous things through it. But that does not make it any less painful, disorienting, and difficult. I see you, and I feel for you. What I have learned about grief has come through God working with unyielding tenderness in the dark moments of my life. I hope to offer a few words of encouragement that will remind you God is doing the exact same thing in your life.

My best friend was electrocuted on a sunny June afternoon in 1982. You might have to reread the previous sentence which does *not* say he was executed (as I thought I heard my mother tell me), but he was electrocuted. An accident to be sure. One born of simple teenage hubris as so many young deaths are.

Toward the close of Steve's funeral, which was open casket, I was the last before the family to file past his body saying goodbye. As I stood over the casket, looking into his face, I put my hands on his chest. As I did, I felt what can only be described as dark cloud, like a growing thunderstorm welling up in my body. It scared me so much that I instinctively did the worst possible thing in trying to stuff and push those feelings back. An action that would have a lasting impact on my emotions for seven years. I was sixteen at the time and would become a true disciple of Jesus Christ at age twenty-one. Although I did not fully realize it then, I became a Christian in mind only. There was not heart. Not for my sin nor in response more importantly to God's love. In studying the Bible, I intellectually accepted that Jesus is the Messiah, my sin put him on the cross, and that salvation was available for me only through Jesus's death, burial, and resurrection. I confessed and repented all my sins. I saw the need for my baptism and willingly did so. But all without heart and vulnerability, because I had closed that door to my emotions that day at Steve's funeral. It would be another two years before someone in my life began asking me some honest and probing questions about why I did not cry. Not at funerals, not in movies, not in pain—never. There was something wrong, but I didn't know it. It took a loving brother to stop and notice that was not a healthy behavior. Oh, that we might look out for each other as Mike Pierce did for me!

So what would I offer you?

- Grieve out loud. There is not a right way to grieve, but there are wrong ways. Stuffing it does not work. Self-medicating with drug and alcohol does not work. Doing it alone and in isolation does not work. But to talk and laugh and grieve in the presence of a few who love you does. That is one bit of advice I would share with myself if I could go back to the funeral with my hand on Steve's chest. Let it out and keeping letting it out, because the storm that was building in me does not last forever.

- Do something comfortable and familiar as it can meet a need for stability. I found myself finding unusual comfort and peace in going to see baseball games. Not professional ones, mind you, but little league games where I did not know a single kid playing, nor any of the friends or family in the bleachers. The subtle rhythms of the game brought a peace that allowed me to process my feelings. Even now I cannot tell you all the reasons why. But I can tell you it brought calm to my heart and mind. Whether it be gardening, walking, building, fishing, or whatever, find your thing and make time for it.

- Look out for those you love. Ask about significant losses in others and put those losses on your prayer list. Vice versa, be sure to let those in your life know of the journey you are on and invite them to show up and help you walk it for a while.

Finally, I would offer one thought from the life of Job. Yes, *that* Job! I can assure the book is so much richer and more meaningful than most understand, but I draw your attention to Job 1:20.

Job has just received four awful reports in what seems to be rapid succession:

> All of Job's oxen and donkeys are stolen by a raiding party of Sabeans. Everyone one of the servants were killed except for 1 to deliver the news. (Job 1:14–15)

> Job's sheep and servants seemed capriciously burned up from a fire of God which fell from the sky. (Job 1:16)

> The entirety of Job's Camel herd is stolen by a different group of folks knows as the Chaldeans with the same enormous loss of life as the Sabeans. (Job 1:17)

> And certainly, the most mortifying and incomprehensible is the loss of his children killed by a sudden and 'might wind.' (Job 1:18–19)

Understandably Job would have been devastated by such tremendous loss. His response is therefore a bit curious in verse 20 where we read "Job got up, tore his robe, and shaved his head. Then he fell to the ground in worship and said: "Naked I came from my mother's womb, and naked I will depart. The LORD gave and the LORD has taken away; may the name of the LORD be praised."

Job mourned indeed, but differently than his surrounding culture did. He did not cut or gash or tattoo himself for the dead as was the common practice among those ancient peoples (Leviticus 19:28). But fell to the ground in worship. What does that mean?

I would suggest it was *not* a joyful expression of song, but rather an acknowledgment that God is God and Job was not. I think it describes a posture of trust and waiting. Almost as if Job is saying to God "I do not know what you are doing or what I should do next. But I will stop, l will listen and wait for you to tell me what I should next. In the midst of his mourning, Job's affirmation of who God is described as worship. When we wait, when we trust, when we are open, and when we offer even our deepest grief to God, this can be considered an act of worship.

I found that the act of worship (acknowledging God as God) and practicing the act of slowing my mind allowing me to think about God and my loss and listening for God's voice was meaningful in ways that I am still discovering.

Additional scriptures for study that have become very meaningful to me:

  Matthew 6:25–33
  John 16:33
  Psalm 34:4–10, 17–18
  John 11:35

F. Wade Cook Jr., L.P.C.
San Diego, CA

NOTES

Title
I Have Seen God's *Care*

Definition: the provision of what is necessary for the health, welfare, maintenance, and protection of someone or something

Theme scripture: 1 Peter 5:7

> "Cast all your anxiety on him because he cares for you."

My dad passed away from a stroke on the third of July. He was sixty-three. He was playing with our dog on the living room floor. He told me the week before he'd never felt healthier. We made it home in time to see him and say goodbye. Thank you, God, for caring for me as I flew home.

After the funeral was over and the whirlwind of hugs and caterers and funeral homes and eulogies and the awkward greeting line where no one knows the right thing to say finally passed by, we finally had our first moment to breathe and be still. The first thing I saw, in the corner of my old bedroom, was a small, window air-conditioning unit. Our home did not have central air, and every summer, Dad would install a few window units. This was his intended weekend project.

It was up to me and my dad's best friend from college, Tom, to complete the task. I've never installed air-conditioning units before, but how hard can it be?

The unit had a piece of paper taped to it, "Mikey's room." There was a small plastic baggie wrapped around the extension cord by a rubber band. Inside the baggie were three screws and a small metal corner fastener. Classic Dad.

Tom stood outside. We took out the screen, opened the window, propped the air conditioner on the window sill, and shut the window as low as it would go. One screw went on the upper right corner of the unit; another screw went on the upper left corner. We let go. Slowly...and...it stayed! Piece of cake!

But my self-satisfaction lasted only a second... I had in my hand one extra screw and a corner fastener that my dad intentionally left in this small plastic baggie wrapped around the extension cord by a rubber band. What was it for? Where did it go? Why did I need it? Why did he leave this for me? Why did *he* leave? Would everything be this difficult now without him?

It didn't go on the bottom of the unit. It didn't go on the side. It all looked held in place pretty nicely. I had no idea what this last piece was for.

Tom, from outside, muffled through the window and said, "Maybe up there?" He pointed up. And sure enough, there was a little hole already screwed into the top of the window. This fastener screwed in so a would-be robber wouldn't be able to open up the bottom window from the outside and sneak in. Classic Dad.

That last piece screwed in perfectly.

Part of me thinks Dad left us early because he left us with everything we need to know; now he wanted to watch us do it on our own—sometimes with a little help from his friends. His planning ahead was my dad's way of caring for me.

God plans ahead. God does that for us all the time. Romans 8:28 reads, "And we know that in all things God works for the good of those who love him, who have been called according to his purpose." Second Peter 1:3 reads, "His divine power has given us everything we need for a godly life through our knowledge of him who called us by his own glory and goodness."

God has given us everything we need. Everything we need. Everything. God cares for you.

Of course, not on your own. You can't do it on your own. Don't ever think you can do it on your own. Why even try?

Paul Tripp has a beautiful entry in his book *New Morning Mercies* about God speaking to Job. "Where were you when I laid the foundation of the earth?"

If you need to be humbled, read the whole thing in Job 38.

> Let your heart take in the grandeur of God's wisdom and power. Let your soul rest in jaw-dropping awe of his majesty. Then remember your own smallness and frailty. Let yourself be humbled by how little you know and how few things you are able to do. Begin to embrace the utterly laughable irrationality of ever thinking that in any situation, location, or relationship it would ever be possible for you to be smarter than God...and in humble gratitude, bow down and worship. (Paul Tripp)

What an amazing God. But what's even better?

He "shut in the sea with doors when it burst out from the womb" *and* he cares for you. He measured the length of the earth and sky *and* he cares for you.

He laid the cornerstones of the earth and universe *and* he cares for you.

My dad knew how to properly install a window unit. God knows how to do everything. He cares for you.

Grab onto God and never let go. He is the father. You are his child.

He cares for you.

Applications:

WRITE DOWN five ways God has cared for you in the past. This is the easiest task that pays the biggest dividends that people do the least. You have to write it down. It makes all the difference. Be on the lookout for one way God cares for you each day.

Just ask Elijah, God often speaks in a whisper. He can speak in a whisper because he is close. Acts 17:27 reads, "He is not far from each one of us." Remove a specific distraction from your life (for 99 percent of us, that's an app on your phone, for instance). Let God fill that space and listen. He will be there. He cares for you.

For further study:

Deuteronomy 31:6
Psalm 23.1–3
Psalm 24: 17–18
Psalm 32.8
Isaiah 40:11
Isaiah 41:13
Isaiah 51:12
Ephesians 2:13

Mike Slater
San Diego, CA

NOTES

Title

I Have Seen God's *Discipline*

Definition: to train or develop by instruction
Theme scripture: Hebrews 12:9–11

> Moreover, we have all had human fathers who disciplined us and we respected them for it. How much more should we submit to the Father of spirits and live! They disciplined us for a little while as they thought best; but God disciplines us for our good, in order that we may share in his holiness. No discipline seems pleasant at the time, but painful. Later on, however, it produces a harvest of righteousness and peace for those who have been trained by it.

Here, the author compares and contrasts our earthly fathers with God as our father. When I think about God's discipline, though challenging at times, it seems understandable and fairly processable; the fact that God is working for the good, and the outcome will be good if I stick with it, persevere, and keep going. It's verse 9, however, and the beginning of verse 10, the part about our earthly fathers, "They disciplined us for a little while as they thought best," that has left me guessing, confused, and heartbroken.

Back in August 2011, I received a call from my oldest sister, very shaken up, she tells me that a small plane crashed in New Jersey and they think it was my dad's (he had been flying for about twenty years).

Silence.

This is the nightmare call for kids of parents who fly planes...

My sister is crying as she is talking to me. I lose it, breaking down and in a state of shock.

My dad, who I just spent the week with, is now dead and I will never see him, be with him, or hear from him again.

Gone. Forever.

Loss. Confusion. No goodbye. No last words.

Unfinished conversations to be had.

Unspoken words to be said.

Unfinished bridges to be built.

Almost nine years now since he passed.

I am not sure if there is a proper way to grieve, or any way to prepare for it.

So many conflicting emotions—gratitude, anger, regret, hurt, sadness, respect.

Like many fathers in my dad's generation, saying "I love you" was not normal or highly practiced.

Nor was "I am proud of you."

I never heard either at forty-four years old when he passed.

The Bible says that our dads did what they thought best. My dad's thinking was to tell me at a young age that I did not have what it takes to be successful.

That way, I would spend my life proving him wrong, which would assure "success."

He played this method all the way to the end. There was always something more to attain.

I set out to prove him wrong in everything that I was involved in. Didn't matter what it was, I was going to win. I was going to win his approval "someday." That was the goal/dream.

Looking back, I am amazed at how God has disciplined me through the "grief journey."

I would love to be able to tell you I "endured hardship as discipline," but that would not be honest.

It has been awkward... What if you don't respect the way your dad raised you? What if it is hard to believe that your dad did what they though best?

I have experienced love, gratitude, appreciation, anger, doubt, resentment, guilt, and regret.

Through it all, God has disciplined me. It has taken *years*, but I can finally say that he has granted me peace—the peace that he promises.

The grieving process has matured me. I believe God has showed me how to accept this verse and believe from the bottom of my heart that my dad really did what he thought was best, and it was my cowardice, my lack of speaking up that hurt the relationship that ended so tragically on that hot August day.

God has been patient with me, as it is has taken me many years to own up to my side of the "dysfunction."

His discipline has showed me how blame and shame are long and winding roads that go nowhere but confusion and guilt.

His discipline has showed me that a bit of anger and conflict are good in relationships and to not be afraid of simply starting a conversation that you are scared to start. To not have to have it "all figured out" before it starts. Simply get the ball rolling...

I do this all with *grace*, knowing that grieving is a wild ride, a sloppy process filled with tears, smiles, reflection, and understanding.

For further study:

> Hebrews 12:4–7
> Romans 5:3–5
> James 1:2–4

Dave Mitchell
Randolph, NJ

NOTES

Title
I Have Seen God's *Empathy*

Definition: intellectual identification with or vicarious experiencing
of the feelings, thoughts, or attitudes of another person
Theme scripture: Romans 5:6–8

> You see, at just the right time, when we were still
> powerless, Christ died for the ungodly. Very rarely
> will anyone die for a righteous man, though for
> a good man someone might possibly dare to die.
> But God demonstrates his own love for us in this:
> While we were still sinners, Christ died for us.

In the summer of 1993, my wife Suzanne was diagnosed with
an aggressive form of cancer. She was admitted to the hospital, and
one month later, passed away. I was left with two boys, one two years
old and the other nine months old. Suddenly, I had to learn how
to take care of two small boys by myself. I had to figure out how to
feed them, to clothe them, and to help them when they were sick. I
remember they both got chicken pox at the same time, and I had to
nurse them both through that experience. It was a challenging time
in my life, to say the least, but with the help of God and the church,
I was able to make it through.

Since everything happened so fast, it took me a few months to
really process/think about things. I thought about Romans 5 and
how the Bible says that God demonstrates his own love for us by
allowing Christ to die on the cross for us.

28

I had always seen how Christ's sacrifice for us showed his love for us, but this passage says that it also shows God's love for us because he had to watch his son suffer and die and do nothing about it.

I remember sitting beside Suzanne's bed in the hospital and feeling powerless. I would sit there and watch her breathe and see the medicine go in and knew that I had no power to change her situation. It was a very humbling feeling. I knew that if I could take her place, I would, but I didn't have the power to do that. All I could do was sit there and watch her suffer and eventually die.

When I thought about Romans 5, I realized that God knew what it meant to watch a loved one suffer.

It made me feel so much closer to God because I knew he could relate to the feelings I had. He knew what it felt like to watch someone you love suffer and not do anything about it. He could empathize with how I felt, and that brought my heart so much closer to God.

What really impacted me, though, was realizing that God could have stopped Jesus's suffering if he wanted to, but he didn't because he knew that I would never have a chance for eternal life if Jesus did not die for my sins. It really showed me God's love for me, because he allowed himself to go through incredible emotional pain by watching his son suffer and die. I loved Suzanne, but nowhere near as much as God loved his one and only son. There is no way I could relate to the amount of pain God must have felt, and yet he went through it for my sake. I know that I could not have done it. If I could have stopped Suzanne's suffering, I would have, but God held back in spite of how he felt so that I could be saved. What tremendous love God has for me and for mankind.

God worked in my life in an amazing way through the experience of losing my spouse. It deepened my trust in him. I always somehow knew God would take care of me and my boys. As I meditated on what happened and how God was with me, I felt so much closer and connected with God than I ever had been before. It brought me in touch with my emotions, and I felt things more deeply, which made me a better friend to people going through hard times, because I knew how it felt. I marvel at how much God loves us.

He was willing to endure the pain of letting his son die because of his love for us.

God definitely took care of me and my boys. I got so much support from the disciples in my region of the San Diego Church of Christ. They helped me learn to be a single dad of two and supported us in so many ways. Several months after my wife died, I began to date, and sooner than I ever thought possible, God led me to my second wife, Mary. We were married about nineteen months after Suzanne passed away. She had two kids of her own from a previous marriage. God blessed our blended family in a tremendous way. We had our challenges, but God worked through them all, and our kids really grew to love our family, and we really don't think of ourselves as blended. We are just family.

No matter how tough the times are you go through, God knows how you feel. He can relate to whatever pain you experience. Let that draw you close to God's heart. Remember 1 Peter 5:7

"Cast all your anxiety on him because he cares for you."

Further scriptures for study:

II Cor. 1:3–7
Ps 139:1–4
Ps. 103:13–18
Heb 4:14–16

Dave Atkins
Redondo Beach, CA

NOTES

Title
I Have Seen God's *Empathy*

Definition: understanding and entering into another's feelings
Theme scripture: John 11: 17–37:

> On his arrival, Jesus found that Lazarus had already been in the tomb for four days. (John 11: 17)

> Now Bethany was less than two miles[b] from Jerusalem, and many Jews had come to Martha and Mary to comfort them in the loss of their brother. When Martha heard that Jesus was coming, she went out to meet him, but Mary stayed at home. (John 11:18–20)

> 'Lord,' Martha said to Jesus, 'if you had been here, my brother would not have died. But I know that even now God will give you whatever you ask.' (John 11:21–22)

> Jesus said to her, "Your brother will rise again." (John 11:23)

> Martha answered, "I know he will rise again in the resurrection at the last day. (John 11:24)

> Jesus said to her, "I am the resurrection and the life. The one who believes in me will live, even

though they die; and whoever lives by believing in me will never die. Do you believe this?" (John 11:25–26)

'Yes, Lord,' she replied, 'I believe that you are the Messiah, the Son of God, who is to come into the world.' (John 11:27)

After she had said this, she went back and called her sister Mary aside. "The Teacher is here," she said, "and is asking for you." When Mary heard this, she got up quickly and went to him. Now Jesus had not yet entered the village, but was still at the place where Martha had met him. When the Jews who had been with Mary in the house, comforting her, noticed how quickly she got up and went out, they followed her, supposing she was going to the tomb to mourn there. (John 11:28–31)

When Mary reached the place where Jesus was and saw him, she fell at his feet and said, 'Lord, if you had been here, my brother would not have died.' (John 11:32)

When Jesus saw her weeping, and the Jews who had come along with her also weeping, he was deeply moved in spirit and troubled. 34 "Where have you laid him?" he asked. 'Come and see, Lord,' they replied. (John 11:33–34)

Jesus wept. (John 11:35)

Then the Jews said, 'See how he loved him!' (John 11:36)

But some of them said, 'Could not he who opened the eyes of the blind man have kept this man from dying?' (John 11:37)

Our God made each one of us, but he made each one of us unique. You are handmade by God, his workmanship, his masterpiece, his unique design. We all have different pasts, different strengths, different demons, but ultimately there is a piece inside each of us that is like him. Grieving is no exception. We do not all grieve the same. The perfection of God is evident in his ability to empathize with each one of us in our moments of weakness as we grieve (Hebrews 4:14–15). As we each grieve differently, God empathizes. He is not confused or stumped by our grief or the ways it manifests. When he looks into our grieving hearts, he understands perfectly. Our God is perfect, even in his ability to handle the deepest waters of our hearts, a task that seems insurmountable in times of grief.

On October 26, 2007, in an instant, without warning, we lost the greatest woman we have ever known—our mother. Jennifer had gone out to dinner with our parents. As they were coming back home, our mom walked through the door, collapsed, and went into sudden cardiac arrest. After hours of fighting to keep her alive, she died. She was our safe place, our best friend, the rock and anchor of our family. Suddenly, she was gone, and it turned our worlds upside down. Our family would never be the same. Even though we were raised in the same home, and believed in the love of the same God, there was nothing the same about how we each responded to this pain.

When asked to write this chapter, we both immediately thought of the story of two sisters, Martha and Mary. The story surrounding the death of their brother, Lazarus, gave us great comfort. Their very different responses to their brother's death resonated with our personal experiences.

Jen's personal story

I am grateful that Lazarus had two sisters, because in Martha, I find a kindred spirit. In the weeks and months that followed my mother's death, I found my heart becoming increasingly troubled by my mourning "journey." And a journey it is! When it comes to emotions, I am more of my mother's daughter, and in my time of greatest emotional need, she was not there. Knowing that the person I needed the most was the one I was grieving for was heart-wrenching. With good motive, people began to express concern over my lack of tearful expressions, questioning whether or not I was allowing myself to grieve. To my great frustration, I found myself more upset by my lack of crying and outward emotions than the loss of my mom! My thoughts included *What's wrong with me? Am I completely emotionally shutdown?* My mom was my best friend, and I thought I loved her deeply; maybe I didn't. Maybe I am doomed to forever be emotionally inept. If I had loved her, I would cry more. I wish I could cry more to show people that *I am* having a hard time. I felt inadequate to respond to people when they asked me how I was doing. It was as though they were searching my eyes for tears, and I had none to give. It turned social settings into seemingly daunting tasks that I found myself dreading.

I will never forget the night I read about these sisters and Jesus. Jesus takes me right where I am! He didn't cry with Martha. She needed answers, and that's what he gave her. He didn't rebuke her for a lack of emotion or even for her questions. He loved her as she was. He tended to her unique emotional needs. What a relief! What freedom! God created our hearts; he knows all the deep waters. He is the most qualified to "draw them out" (Proverbs 20). He taught me along the way how to grow in areas where I was weak. He taught me about vulnerability and the power of letting others into our darkest places. As Martha, we must go to *him* for answers. I am comforted by Jesus's own questions on the cross, in a time of great pain and despair (Matthew 27:46). I had a lot of questions for God. Many months were spent camping out on scriptures about his goodness and love. Every day, I would read them and pray that God would help me to believe them. We will not find answers to our questions anywhere else. I had heard over and over that each person grieves differently, and yet it took me a long time to discover the peace that comes with knowing that God understands *me* perfectly. Jesus is the true meaning of empathy.

Leslie's personal story

Let's just say that Mary was not as composed as Martha. She fell at Jesus's feet. She wept. When she ran to Jesus, the crowd who had gathered to mourn with her followed. I wonder if they thought she might flip out. I was pretty similar. My grief was not hidden—I was angry and emotional. It was visible, out in the open, for all to see. My need for comfort was obvious to those around me, just as it was with Mary. I know people around me were concerned. My grief, unlike Jesus's when he was in pain, was not without sin. I lashed out at people. I accused God. I felt like he had not kept his promises.

In the same way that I know Jesus could have rebuked Mary for her unbelief and her shallow faith, God would have been just in doing the same to me. However, he doesn't correct her, rebuke her, or teach her. He saw through her sin and saw her pain. He wanted to be with her in her place of pain. We see him doing the same thing throughout the gospels. He saw through the calloused heart and guarded walls of the Samaritan woman's pain (John 4:1–38). He saw through the wild and risky behavior of the adulterous woman (John 8:1–11). He saw through all of my mess and saw my pain—it was here that he loved me.

Gosh, there was such relief in knowing that he did not take offense, that he was not insecure, and that he didn't expect me to "snap out of it" or "pull it together." In Luke 7:11–17, we see a mother in such deep pain that she neither saw Jesus nor believed in him (both of which could be considered a sin). Jesus, however, had such compassion for her that he healed her son without her even asking. His heart also goes out to us in our time of weakness. Jesus knew that in loving me this way, his love would lead my heart not only toward healing but also to repentance.

Jesus saw that these sisters had different needs. He comforted Martha by answering her questions and comforted Mary by weeping with her. He is not afraid of your grief (however it manifests). He is not afraid of the dark place you are in. It does not scare him off. He is wise. Our perfect God knows how to empathize with us in our weakness.

Applications:

- To help you understand God's empathy, find scriptures that show how you are like God when you grieve.
- Write down all your fears and concerns about your grieving heart, and then one by one, pray through them. As you pray, thank God that he knows exactly how to help you through each one. Allow his word to put your heart at rest that he can keep you on solid ground as you weather the storms.

Further study:

Exodus 34:6–7
Psalm 103
Psalm139:14
Psalm 34:18
Isaiah 42:3

Jennifer Ottenweller Chiles and Leslie Ottenweller Karamitas
Atlanta, GA

NOTES

Title
I Have Seen God's *Encouragement*

Definition: giving courage, confidence, and hope
Theme scripture: Genesis 45:8

> So then, it was not you who sent me here, but
> God. He made me father to Pharaoh, lord of his
> entire household and ruler of all Egypt.

There are so many lessons we can learn from the life of Joseph, son of Jacob. He is an inspirational example of faith, forgiveness, compassion, and perseverance. His righteousness is amazing. But I wanted to focus on how God's encouragement helped him to stay righteous through the hardships he endured. God was there through every one of his trials, inspiring, helping, and putting courage into Joseph.

God began encouraging Joseph during his childhood. In Genesis 37:1–11, we learn how his earthly father favored him over his other sons. Joseph must have felt secure in his father's love. Joseph was also given a special talent from God that enabled him to interpret dreams. And he was the best-dressed shepherd in Canaan.

However, there was a downside to these gifts. His brothers were jealous and sinned against him in a treacherous way. Most of them even considered murdering him. They settled for stripping him of his beautiful robe, throwing him in a cistern and selling him into slavery (Genesis 37:12–36).

Many times, God gives us encouraging gifts, but because of our sin or the sin of others, these blessings can seem negative. Sometimes we feel that all of the good has been completely erased by the bad. But God will give us more encouragement and additional talents if we follow Joseph's example and stay close to him.

For Joseph, the encouragement from God continued just as the mistreatment continued. He was blessed in all he did for a time, earning the complete trust of his owner, Potiphar, the captain of the guard (Genesis 39:1–20). And even though Joseph was worthy of that trust, he was falsely accused of rape by Potiphar's wife and thrown into prison. He suffered another crushing blow! But again, God encouraged Joseph while he was in prison. He had the favor of the prison warden and was given responsibility for all that was done at the prison (Genesis 39:21–23). Also, he was able to use his talent for interpreting dreams, and he correctly interpreted the dreams of the baker and the cupbearer (Genesis 40). Joseph was handed another disappointment when the cupbearer forgot about him. It seemed as though Joseph had not received any benefit from this talent.

However, after two years, when Pharaoh had two puzzling dreams, the cupbearer remembered him. God encouraged Joseph by causing Pharaoh to have these dreams that only Joseph could interpret. God made these dreams incredibly important to the future of everyone in that part of the world. As a result, Joseph was put in charge of the palace—second only to the Pharaoh (Genesis 41).

Then God continued to encourage him as he was put in charge of Egypt and saved the lives of countless people with his plan to store up food before the famine. Joseph is finally reunited with his family and forgives his brothers for their horrible crimes toward him (Genesis 42–44). Joseph knew that it was God's plan all along, and I believe that God's encouragement helped him to stay strong and righteous (Genesis 45:4–8).

Joseph's trials are different than mine. However, we both suffered tremendous losses because of someone else's sin. He and I both know the pain of someone's hate impacting our lives and changing them forever. But Joseph seems to go through his struggles in a very godly way. The Bible doesn't mention him struggling emotionally or with faithlessness as he went through these trials. Well, I think that he must have struggled in some way. However, I believe that he got to a place of faith and encouragement faster than many of us do. It was very hard for me to get to that place when I went through a very traumatic situation years ago. But God helped to get there! Here is my story...

I am originally from St. Louis, Missouri. I grew up in a nice suburban neighborhood with basically no crime. I was an only child with two wonderful parents who were well-educated, had a great marriage, were involved in church, and were involved in tons of community organizations. It seems rare these days, but I had a wonderful childhood, and although I'd always wished for brothers and sisters, I had tons of aunts, uncles, and cousins around. We took a lot of family vacations around the country, and for some reason, I fell in love with New York City. So, despite my family and friends thinking I was crazy to want to live in such a dangerous city, my parents paid for me to go to New York University. I graduated with a degree in journalism, and that same year, I was reached out to by someone from the New York City Church of Christ, known as the Central Park Church of Christ back then. I was baptized a few months after that.

So fast-forward five years. I was working in a fun job and living with three other sisters in Christ—each from a different Caribbean country. It was Wednesday, December 20, and I was supposed to fly home to St. Louis for Christmas on Friday, the twenty-second. I'd always gone home for Christmas since I'd lived in New York. I was working at my desk, and my boss came up to me. She said that she needed to talk to me and the executive director. She was shaking and very upset. I thought I'd done something wrong. On the way up to the executive director's office, in the elevator, she told me that my parents had been shot. My dad was dead, and my mom was in a coma in the hospital. I went into immediate shock and denial, I think. But I just felt numb, and I didn't react emotionally. I usually don't react right away in times of crisis; the emotions come out later for some reason. The executive director had me talk to a detective on the phone from St. Louis. He asked me if I had any idea who might have done this, and all I could think of was an eighteen-year-old boy whose family had recently moved across the street. My parents had told me that he was causing trouble in the neighborhood and that all the neighbors were having a tough time dealing with him.

The next few days were a blur. I went back to St. Louis with one of my roommates. Eventually, all of my roommates plus some other friends from church came to St. Louis to be with me. I remember praying constantly. I did not want to think. I just prayed from second to second, "God be with me, help me," etc. I don't remember much else. My relatives were there from everywhere. They were amazing and took care of so much because I was just so out of it. I did get to see my mom in the hospital, and it helped to see her still breathing even though she was in a coma and on life support. She was basically gone, though, and on the twenty-third, she passed away.

It was very surreal to me. I handled things in a very detached way. I think that's because I was in shock and denial. Also, because I hadn't ever had to deal with that much trauma. Before this happened, I would avoid any emotional pain by stuffing or burying it deep in my mind. I was used to being happy, so I would avoid any unhappiness as much as possible. However, the emotional pain would usually resurface at a later time when triggered by some other difficult situation.

So when I went through this horrible event, I may have subconsciously buried my feelings—not on purpose, but because it was the only way I could deal with it. But I knew that I needed to deal with the pain somehow. And as a Christian, I believed in prayer. So I prayed...almost constantly. I wouldn't allow myself to think, afraid that I would spiral down into negativity, depression, or insanity. I remember praying from one second to the next, just continually talking to God.

My wonderful relatives continued to help me with all of the estate planning and funeral planning. I never had imagined that I'd have to plan a double funeral for my parents. But the help was there from relatives and disciples that came to comfort me from New York. I did not know many disciples from the St. Louis church at the time, but some of them were at the funeral, and they offered to help in any way that they could. The funeral was a big event since my parents were well-known and well-loved in the community. There was

42

a police escort and a lot of people. But I felt utterly alone, and I very seldom feel lonely. As an only child, I was used to being by myself, and I usually enjoyed it. But it was as if all my physical connection to this world was gone, and even though I had other relatives and my spiritual family, I still felt isolated.

But I continued to pray. And as I think back, there were many encouraging things from God. He'd put it on my heart to live in New York City where I found the church that has been encouraging me to this day. He allowed me to be in New York when it happened so that I did not have to experience it firsthand. God had given me many wonderful, well-educated, and financially talented relatives who came to help right away with everything. He'd given me five years in the church to cultivate a deep relationship with him and the Bible. He'd given me many spiritual friends—several who traveled back to St. Louis with me. He'd allowed me to see my mom while she was still breathing and say goodbye. He'd allowed me to have twenty-eight years to be loved, raised, and taught by the most awesome parents in the world. Also, they caught the guy that did it. It was the neighbor boy. Many people in the neighborhood suspected him, and they caught him when he tried to use one of my dad's credit cards at a store. It was a relief and an encouragement from God to know that they caught the person who did this and that he is serving a life sentence in prison with no chance of parole.

Also, something amazing happened when I was in St. Louis staying with my cousin Jerri and her two daughters, Tonja and Tanjila. I think this was before the funeral, but I don't remember. I asked Tonja to pick something from the Bible for me to read. She was about nine, and she picked one of the few things that would've encouraged me at that time. It was totally God, because she had no idea what it said. She just picked it randomly because she thought it said "job," and she thought that was interesting. It was Job 42:10–12. That gave me hope.

Then something even more amazing happened. A few days before the funeral, my uncle Robert said, "I'm going to shock you." I was already in shock, so I thought *okay*. He's one of my dad's brothers, and they were very close. He said, "You have a brother." He told me that my dad had a son before he met my mom. He wasn't married to the woman, so they kept it quiet, and no one knew except some of my older relatives. Then my dad met my mom, they got married, and had me. My dad told my mom, but he didn't know how I'd take it. (Of course, I would've been happy because I'd always wanted brothers and sisters.) My uncle thought that my dad would want me to know under the circumstances, and he invited my brother to the funeral and wanted me to meet him ahead of time. He told me that my brother, Jimmy, had a wife and two kids. So I got to meet him and found out that he was a part-time preacher at a traditional Church of Christ in Abilene, Texas. We bonded instantly. He had actually known about me all along because he'd kept in contact with my dad. So I went from being a daughter to being a sister and an aunt. I didn't feel so alone and isolated anymore. What an encouragement from God!

In mid-January of 1990, I came back to New York. The disciples were really there for me in a great way. And even though the tragedy didn't happen in New York, I decided I needed a change. I felt that I wanted to be in a sunny place; so I prayed, and God put San Diego on my heart. I am so grateful that God encouraged me to make the decision to move here. He has been encouraging me through that decision every day.

Of course, there have been times when I have broken down in tears and felt deep sadness since they've been gone. Other difficult events—like the loss of other family members and friends, some terrible world events, and even a breakup with one of my boyfriends—has triggered the pain I felt when my parents were killed. And I still miss them and wonder what my life would have been like if they were still alive. I still feel a sadness on special days, like their birthdays, anniversary, Christmas, Mother's and Father's Day, etc. But I have grown in going to God first and praying through the pain before allowing myself to fall into the downward spiral of negativity and faithlessness. More and more, I also feel a peace that really does transcend understanding. I have a special photo of them in my room that gives me joy, and I have wonderful visits with them in my dreams. I believe that through all of the encouragement God has given me, I have been able to stay faithful to him and have a very fulfilled and purposeful life.

For further study:

> But you, O God, do see trouble and grief; you consider it to take it in hand. The victim commits himself to you; you are the helper of the fatherless. (Psalm 10:14–18)

> The Lord Himself goes before you and will be with you; He will never leave you nor forsake you. Do not be afraid. Do not be discouraged. (Deuteronomy 31:8–9)

> The eyes of the Lord are on the righteous and his ears are attentive to their cry; the face of the Lord is against those who do evil, to cut off the memory of them from the earth. The righteous cry out, and the Lord hears them; he delivers them from all their troubles. The Lord is close to the brokenhearted and saves those who are crushed in spirit. (Psalm 34:15–18)

> Have I not commanded you? Be strong and courageous. Do not be terrified; do not be discouraged, for the Lord your God will be with you wherever you go. (Joshua 1:9)

Lori Frederick
San Diego, CA

NOTES

Title

I Have Seen God's *Faithfulness*

Definition: steadfast in affection or allegiance; firm in adherence to
  promises; given with strong assurance
Theme scripture: Psalm 40:10

> Do not withhold your mercy from me, Lord; may
> your love and faithfulness always protect me.

God's faithfulness is evident throughout Scripture. One of the best examples of his faithfulness was with the children of Israel. Let me paraphrase (if you have tweens or teens, this may sound familiar):

'We're SICK of making bricks and being slaves, please save us!' So God prepares Moses to lead the Israelites out of bondage in Egypt. All the Israelites did just what the LORD had commanded Moses and Aaron. And on that very day the LORD brought the Israelites out of Egypt by their divisions (Exodus 12:50–51).

Almost immediately, they began to grumble 'we're thirsty!' God's response in Exodus 15:25 was "Then Moses cried out to the LORD, and the LORD showed him a piece of wood. He threw it into the water, and the water became fit to drink."

Next, they whined, 'If only we had died in Egypt—at least there we had all we wanted to eat, now we're STARVING.' God's response in Exodus 16:8 was "Moses also said, 'You will know that it was the LORD when he gives you meat to eat in the evening and all the bread you want in the morning, because he has heard your grumbling against him. Who are we? You are not grumbling against us, but against the LORD.'

Then they say "Moses has been gone too long, make us gods to go before us." Aaron followed the people's request. God was angry and ready to destroy them, but Moses pleaded on their behalf, and again, God's faithfulness is shown in Exodus 32:14: "Then the LORD relented and did not bring on his people the disaster he had threatened."

Later, we hear them again complaining about their situation, ignoring all the times God has faithfully cared and provided for them. They say "We want a king like all the other nations." In 1 Samuel 8:7–9, we hear God say "And the LORD told him: 'Listen to all that the people are saying to you; it is not you they have rejected, but they have rejected me as their king. As they have done from the day I brought them up out of Egypt until this day, forsaking me and serving other gods, so they are doing to you. Now listen to them; but warn them solemnly and let them know what the king who will reign over them will claim as his rights.' But again, God relented, and God responds in 1 Samuel 8:22: "The LORD answered, 'Listen to them and give them a king.'"

God faithfully loved his people then and continues to do so to this day. His faithfulness was never more evident in my life than in the 1980s. I was raised as a "preacher's kid," graduated from a "Christian College," and taught one year in a Christian academy. Then I walked away from my relationship with God for about ten years. I moved to Dallas. All my relationships were very worldly. I was the "responsible" one. I had a regular job, a car, paid my bills. I got the calls at two in the morning to drive someone home from a night of partying.

I met David in the early '80s. He was funny, kind, loving, but living with the consequences of a series of bad choices. He'd lived on his own since he was sixteen, been in trouble with the law, had a string of jobs, and been involved with alcohol and street drugs for years. Still, I saw something in him. We became very close, and in 1986, we were living together platonically. He began feeling bad, and we went to a doctor who said "exercise and take vitamins." His health declined, so we saw another doctor who ran some tests. The words still ring in my ear: "David, you are HIV-positive." Very little was known about HIV. People were diagnosed, and some died within months or weeks. We went through shock, denial, anger, and fear.

Within days, I was at church, begging God to forgive me and give me his strength for this journey. I asked the body for forgiveness and for prayers for a difficult situation a friend was going through. God's faithfulness was so evident; I felt his love directly and through the church I began attending.

I was in this for the long haul, and we loved each other. In 1988, we got married and moved to Garland. I found a church home and went for several years alone. There were difficulties along the way. David stopped using drugs before I agreed to marry him. Then occasionally, he'd give in to the stress of the illness, and I would find a used needle or money missing. One day, I looked at him and said, "I will do whatever it takes to get through this with you, but I will not watch you kill yourself. You decide now, me or the drugs." To my knowledge, he never used meth again.

God began to work on David's heart. He pursued him through my faith, his fear, and through some very loving people at church who loved David where he was (God's amazing faithfulness!) He had a great doctor and got into some drug trials (faithfulness). He felt stronger and was working full time. We were optimistic for the first time in a long time.

David began attending worship services with me, and in 1994, he was baptized (FAITHFULNESS!). He became very involved. He gave warm hugs, wrote many cards of encouragement, made meals for others, and helped in the Wednesday night kindergarten class. I remember he wasn't feeling well, but he was on all fours giving "horsey rides" to those precious kids. We found our "tribe" at church who, in addition to a few of the elders, we told about David's illness. They loved and supported us in ways we couldn't imagine. He had reconciled with his family, and they were also loving and supportive.

In 1997, David went on disability. We hoped it would be like other times: a new drug or treatment would make him better. But this time it wasn't to be. Our life became a series of doctor visits, home health, IV infusions, fifty to sixty pills a day. He lost his sight and had trouble walking.

On August 14, 1999, he told me he had been unable to urinate for three days. We called his doctor and immediately went to the ER, and he was admitted. He continued to lose motor skills and was paralyzed from the waist down. We spent seven weeks in Baylor. While we had tremendous love and support, there were times when it was just me, God (faithfulness), and the humming of machines helping him breathe and delivering meds to keep him alive. While he was still lucid, we held hands and relived our life together. I read the Psalms to him. I sat in the darkness with my laptop late at night and wrote his memorial service, my last gift to him. He would want laughter and sharing of memories, and I wanted to be the one to give him that.

Finally, his doctor knew David wasn't going to get better. I sat in his office in tears and told him I wasn't sure I could make the decision to take him off the curative meds alone. He said, "You don't have to. I'm making it with you" (God's faithfulness). I believe David chose to stop eating and drinking—it was the only control he had left.

My younger sister, Kathi, who had lost her husband to leukemia several years earlier, flew in to be with me the last few days of David's life. She could minister to me like no one else (his faithfulness). On Sunday night, I sat in a chair beside his bed and held his hand throughout the night. He hadn't spoken or made any other intentional movements in days. But that night, several times, he squeezed my hand. He was saying goodbye the only way he could. I whispered, "Please let go, I will be okay; save me a place in heaven, and I will meet you there."

At eleven o'clock, Monday morning, September 27, the day before his forty-first birthday, he went home. Our friends took my program and created a beautiful memorial service with many memories and laughter and a celebration lunch. Afterward, we released hundreds of bright, colorful balloons. He would have loved it. I believe he did love it.

I spent two healing weeks with Kathi, reading, praying, meditating, and being ministered to by her family (faithfulness). While I hated his suffering, I was grateful we were able to share our grief and say the things we wanted to say to each other.

I was prepared to spend the rest of my life alone, serving this faithful Father who had carried me through this situation which, though difficult, I wouldn't have traded for anything. However, he had other plans. Just six weeks after David's death, I met Glen. We had worked together for years but had never met in person. Again, God in his faithfulness gave me desires of my heart that I had not even allowed myself to consider. A year and a half later, we were married. Then we became foster parents, and in January of 2003, a little four-year-old girl came to live with us. She was immediately part of our hearts. God is so amazing and FAITHFUL! I fully believe that he chose her for us before she was born. In November 2003, we legally adopted her. This year she turned twenty-one. She is now a wife and mother. While David is still very much a part of my heart, I cannot imagine my life without Glen and Makayla. But even more, I cannot imagine living without my faithful heavenly Father.

As he was faithful throughout Scripture, he continues to be faithful to us today. Watch for his faithfulness in your life... You don't want to miss it.

For further study:

Psalm 86:11
Psalm 91:2
Psalm 100:5
Isaiah 25:1

Suzan Mills
Garland, TX

NOTES

Title
I Have Seen God's *Goodness*

Definition: the beneficial or nourishing element of food
Theme scripture: Psalm 23:6

> Surely your goodness and love will follow me all
> the days of my life and I will dwell in the house
> of the Lord forever.

The goodness and presence of God is evident all over the scriptures as Psalms 34:8 says, "Taste and see that the Lord is good; blessed is the one who takes refuge in him."

God's goodness is so visible throughout the scriptures and in the book of Esther, the story of Mordecai who was a Jew living out his years in exile, and Esther who was an orphan and was raised by Mordecai were both unknown and obscure people living in exile. This story is such a powerful reminder of God's goodness and his presence in times of deep uncertainty and loss. He is absent by name in the book of Esther but is present in every turn and event that happened there. Esther had to be courageous and reach out. Though God may at times seem distant, and though he is invisible to us, he is always present and is at work. He is the God who sees the events of our lives ahead of time and is able to meet us where we are.

My sister Rachel and I became Christians in 1992 and had ever since been the best of friends and shared a bond that grew stronger through the years when we were disciples. We were partners in life and the gospel. Early on in our Christian life, we both went on a mission to help build a small church in South India (Cochin). Later,

Rachel and another sister Candice were two disciples who helped start the church in Kuwait. Candice's husband would drive and pick up visitors, and he later, watching the faith of these two women, went back to the States, studied the Bible, and got baptized. A few years later, my husband and I moved to Kuwait and were able to serve together with Rachel to continue the work that she had begun.

There is something truly special, deep, and bonding to have blood family in the faith. We shared a history of common stories, events, and experiences of our childhood, as well as of our Christian journey together. She lived her life faithfully loving, serving, and giving to the body of Christ. I admired her kind, gentle, and kindred spirit not just toward me but to the body of believers and to anybody who would walk through the church door.

In 2010, she suddenly became very ill, and after a couple of misdiagnoses, she was diagnosed with acute lymphoblastic leukemia, and in 2012, she left for her heavenly abode, leaving behind her four-year-old daughter, Eliana, and husband Jonathan. Her death left a deep sense of loss at losing someone with whom I shared my past and present life. I was filled with worry and anxiety about her daughter, and I felt chocked and struggled to express my grief in words. I was unable to express the loss I felt and began to retreat into myself and suffer alone. I cut myself off from my husband and family. I was unable to pray and would sit for days trying to pray, but the only question I had was "why did she have to go?" I did not know what to do with the grief and pain, and when I had exhausted all my energy and became tired of grieving, many weeks later, I reached out to a sister who was helping me, and she told me something that was so profound that changed the way I looked at my grief and suffering. She told me that I should not let my pain and suffering go in vain. It was then that I was able to take all my grief, pain, and mourning to God. And surely my great and loving heavenly Father opened my eyes and taught me things that only grief can teach. Ecclesiastes 7:2 says that is it better to go to a house of mourning than to go to a house of feasting. Ecclesiastes 7:4 says the heart of the wise is in the house of mourning. God become my teacher, and I learned how I wanted to live and die; joyfully entrusting into God's hands, just like my sister did. I have learned how to be a kindred spirit to those who suffer loss of loved ones. I am also learning to care deeply for my niece and to provide for her emotional needs since the last two years she has been living with me, and we are working on adopting her into our family. At the time of my sister's death, everything was so uncertain, but God who is good and present when we cannot see him is always at work. It is eight years since my sister passed away, but I am still here and so is her daughter, safe and secure in God's loving hands. When I look at Eliana today, I know with certainty that God's goodness and love has followed us all the days of our lives. By faith, we see his goodness and feel his presence, and inaudibly, we hear him in the events of our lives, whether it be the crushing blows or the joyful triumphs of life.

For further study:

> Psalm 23
> Esther 4: 13–16
> Psalm 27:13
> Isaiah 142:7

Jesse Pradeep Kutty
Kuwait

NOTES

Title

I Have Seen God's *Goodness*

Definition: qualities of character or conduct that entitle the possessor
    to approval and esteem; moral excellence, virtue; the best part
    of anything; essence
Theme scripture: Psalm 34:8

> Taste and see that the Lord is good; blessed is the
> man who takes refuge in him.

We all experience tragedy differently. We all grieve differently.
At our worst and perhaps weakest points, with a rapid firing of accu-
satory thoughts, we may question God with: How could this have
happened? Why did *you* allow this to take place? I've been faithful
to you. What did I do to deserve this? Our questioning may even
border on accusing him and questioning his goodness.

It's not that I am above that kind of questioning, but long ago
I *determined to choose* the mindset of trusting *the truth* of God's word
over my feelings, my circumstances, or my understanding. Knowing
myself and how powerful and destructive my thoughts can be, particu-
larly at a time of what seems to be "madness," this decision of trusting
the truth of God's word is the *only* truth of protection that can stand
up against the schemes of Satan and his tormenting of my heart and
mind.

To counter the temptation to question the Lord about his character and what he "allows," I reaffirm to myself his holiness and his
compassion by reading accounts of his goodness. A few of my favor-
ites are in Genesis. I love knowing that it is *God who initiates* and

seeks out Adam and Eve as they were in shame and hiding after disobeying. I am moved seeing the nurturing side of God as he *makes clothing* for Adam and Eve even as he expels them from the garden of Eden in Genesis 3. I am in awe of God as his heart and desire for mankind is revealed as he allows Abraham to make multiple appeals regarding the minimum number of righteous people needed to be found in the city of Sodom in order to turn away God's wrath. That number went from fifty to ten righteous people in Genesis 18. Have you seen the manifestation of God's goodness repeatedly displayed as his nature reveals compassion, justice, and nurturing in the Word and in your life?

For more than ten years, I had been anticipating this phone call. Every time the caller ID showed my mom's phone number, I braced myself as I answered it, expecting to hear "the words." Then on September 18, 2007, around one in the afternoon, the words I dreaded were spoken: "*Thomas is dead.*" Sadness, despair, guilt, and numbness engulfed me. My reality seemed surreal. It was as though the ability to speak and make phone calls, listen to condolences, go through a barrage of pictures for his memorial service, and the ability to console my mom was set on "autopilot." At a time of extreme sorrow and confusion, all I knew to do was to cling to the promises of God: "He is good and he blesses those who take refuge in him."

Thomas was the youngest of us four siblings; I was eleven when Thomas was born. He was a welcome and much-loved addition to our family. By the time I went off to college, the difference between our ages was more apparent; I was unaware of all that was happening in his preteen and teen years. Between our parents' divorce and his entry into middle school, Thomas started experimenting with drugs. It wasn't until he was in his twenties that I realized the seriousness of his addiction. Drugs became a stranglehold and crutch for the remainder of Thomas's life.

Over the course of time, Thomas had a successful job, got married, had two sons, and lost one to SIDS. His marriage dissolved, and he was given primary custody of his son, TJ. As Thomas's drug use increased, it became obvious that he was unable to adequately care for TJ. Given that Steve, my husband, and I had four children close to TJ's age, it was only natural that we offer to help out by raising my brother's son. So at the age of nine, TJ joined our family. It was understood and always the goal for TJ to reunite with his dad once Thomas was drug-free.

It is an emotionally exhausting experience when someone in the family is controlled by a substance. Addiction to any vice produces tumultuous emotional upheavals, especially for those trying to help. Before we knew it, days became weeks, which turned into months, and eventually years, with nothing changing in Thomas's life except for more emotional trauma. Thomas's life as a drug addict became characterized by emotional ups and downs, police calls, arrests, jail, doctors, counseling, ambulances, suicide attempts, drug overdoses, rehabs, breakdowns, and homelessness.

The closest Thomas got to getting his life back was the year he lived at Dunklin, a Christian rehabilitation community in South Florida. At Dunklin, he received counseling, mentoring, and lots of time to reflect on his life and on what he had lost and wanted to reclaim—his son, TJ. His stay at Dunklin was his "about-face." Thomas blossomed, became a leader and led group sessions, developed self-worth and self-esteem, and learned about Jesus. He graduated from the one-year program drug- and cigarette-free. I pleaded that he not return to his hometown, to start over somewhere new to give himself the best possible chance of staying "clean," but my plea fell on deaf ears. It was only a matter of time before the vicious cycle began again. From the lighting of the first cigarette, Thomas relapsed once more into a stranglehold of drugs. Thomas died one and a half years after leaving Dunklin. One day after a night-long drug binge, Thomas's heart simply stopped. We will never know whether his death was intentional or not. He was thirty-eight.

It has now been thirteen years since Thomas's death. That "empty" feeling never really goes away; after all, he was my brother. Thankfully I am not "left to myself" but am assured that only God is equipped to intercede and heal my pain. I am so grateful for the numerous scriptures God provides for me to hold onto in times of troubling emotions. It is only when I see him as my refuge that I can clearly see and experience his goodness.

For further study:

> Psalm 16:8
> Psalm 62
> Psalm 63:1–8
> Psalm 100:5

Sandy Jacoby
St. Augustine, FL
Malpaisillo, Nicaragua

NOTES

Title

I Have Seen God's *Healing*

Definition: to make healthy, whole, or sound; restore to health; free
    from ailment
Theme scripture: Romans 8:28

> And we know that in all things God works for
> the good of those who love him, who have been
> called according to his purpose.

When I got married, I believed that with the good and the bad,
the ups and the downs, if two people loved each other, they could
overcome all things no matter what. This included me thinking I
could change my spouse for the better. You see, my husband was an
alcoholic, he had anger issues, there was verbal and emotional abuse
taking place in our home where we were raising our two sons. There
is a saying that goes something like "The person we marry has the
same level of woundedness as we do." This insight escaped me for
some time because I was so focused on taking care of my husband's
issues. I thought I could change him. I thought I was the answer
to his pain and frustrations. I got very busy working on his issues,
forgetting I had issues of my own. Looking back, one of the biggest
mistakes I had made was I hadn't ever asked him if he wanted or
needed help with his drinking and anger. It didn't even occur to me.
I assumed he'd be in agreement with my plan to save him. This is
where I now see how much I needed my own saving and healing as
well.

I, along with my older brother and younger sister, was raised by my father. He was an alcoholic. He loved us, but he himself was broken and had very few tools to guide us as we grew. This and other life hurts set the stage for patterns of dysfunction that were weaved throughout my life. I remember making statements to myself and others around me that I would never put myself in a position where I would be in this kind of dysfunction. Yet here I found myself married to the same type of craziness that I had been trying to avoid. A few years into our marriage, as things were quickly falling apart, we started to look for solutions.

One of the things we found was a really good church. It was here that I started a deeper walk with God. I enjoyed gaining understanding about who he was and how much love he has for each one of us. With this knowledge, I still spent the first handful of years in the marriage stuck in a dysfunctional cycle of blaming and resenting my husband. I was basing my responses and actions on his degree of "healthiness." When in reality, I had my own level of unhealthiness that I wasn't factoring into the equation. I began to see that part of our life as Christians is allowing God to expose hurts, false thinking, and ungodly reactions to past and current situations that were causing bitterness, fear, and hopelessness. This knowledge put me on a different path in my understanding that God is working all things for my good.

I began to let go of trying to force or control things; but rather, see what God wanted me to learn and grow in. I started speaking differently. Instead of anger and overreaction, I was able to express what I was willing or unwilling to do in my marriage. I began to be free of the demands of another person, instead striving for righteousness. Honoring God and myself allowed me to learn to honor my husband. In my situation, this meant letting him choose if he wanted to change and grow. In fact, who was I to try to make him do anything. Treating him the way Jesus does allows him to have his free will choice. This in turn allowed me to live for God and his righteousness. God became my source of strength. He became the one I would pour my heart out to. Many a night I spent on my knees crying out to him, sharing my pain and heartache, telling him I was willing to surrender to his will and his timing. I found great joy in holding on to God for comfort and guidance.

God began to answer the question I kept bringing to him: "What does a godly wife look like in my situation?" I got better at placing boundaries down. Instead of participating in my part of the dysfunction, I chose to not try to control what I thought would be best for my husband, but allow the natural causes of negative behavior to correct him of the way he was living his life. I had chosen to separate from my husband. His actions and behavior did not match what he and I heard being preached at church each Sunday. We tried marriage counseling. We tried to restore the marriage twice. I was still waiting for all this to be used for the good so my husband and I could start to help other couples in similar situations. All the work we did in counseling I believed would help us get on the same page. I waited for him to win back my trust, to hear my heart, and to walk away from the things I still believed were keeping him from living in freedom in Christ. I thought the pain and frustration over the two decades we were married would be worth it if these things could be obtained. God is more than capable of restoring all of these things. The gift he gave me is accepting every person has the free will to decide for themselves. In this lesson, I found I could love him most like Jesus when I let go of the expectations of what a husband's role was according to the Bible. In the twenty years we were married, he had accumulated four DUIs. That and the continued chaos and discord in our home brought me to a place with God, of begging to be released from my marriage. I saw that unless words and actions match, they cannot keep a marriage afloat. One particular evening, I wept before God, telling him I had given all I had left. I told God I had tried over and over even when I didn't want to try anymore. I told him that I trusted him, and I knew his ways were better than mine. God heard me. Two years later, God revealed and exposed more, and I was released from my marriage covenant and am now divorced.

God has used all of this for the good. I have the privilege of working with women in similar situations. The goal is not to give up or quit on your marriage when things are difficult. The goal is to let God reveal how you are adding to the dysfunction and instead learn to live for God's righteousness. Allowing sin to stay hidden and not dealt with is participating in darkness. God desires his sons and daughters to live free of bondage. He is willing to free us and to heal us. He is waiting for us to invite him in to do so.

When I look back, I am so grateful for all the things that took place. My circumstances compelled me to seek a deep relationship with God. He does not disappoint. He waited patiently for me to bring the broken parts of my heart to him so he could heal and restore those parts and make me whole. He taught me to let go of anger, bitterness, and resentment. They don't serve anyone, and they will destroy everyone. Seeing I wasn't better than my ex-husband, but in need of the same Savior has brought me to a place of deep compassion toward him. I've learned to listen to God's voice above all the others clamoring for my attention. God sent Jesus to be an atonement for our sins, and this is truly amazing, but then to have him be willing to walk with us in the depths of our souls to find healing is beyond what we could ask or imagine. I trust him with every part of me, and I'm willing to put my life in his hands. He is the true healer.

For further study:

> Eph 5:11
> Duet 30:19
> Eph 3:20

Michelle Hitt
Ramona, CA

NOTES

Title
I Have Seen God's *Sovereignty*

Definition: the quality or state of being sovereign, or of having
   supreme power or authority
Theme scripture: Romans 9:21–23

> When a potter makes jars out of clay, doesn't he
> have the right to use the same lump of clay to
> make one jar for decoration and another to throw
> garbage into? In the same way, even though God
> has the right to show his anger and power, he is
> very patient with those on whom his anger falls,
> who are destined for destruction. He does this to
> make the riches of his glory shine even brighter
> on those to whom he shown mercy, who were
> prepared in advance for glory.

I was the young age of twenty-eight years old. My wife and
I first met in high school. She was my one and only. We dated in
high school and through college and then decided to get married.
We were excited about our new life ahead, and she continued to help
me pursue my dreams in aviation. I was hired by a major air carrier;
together we were achieving our goals. By this time, we had been married five years, purchased our first home, and had a son. Soon after,
she became pregnant with our second child.

During the delivery, there were complications. I found myself
in the waiting room of ICU. Late that night, I sat alone. Afraid.
Unsure. Suddenly there was commotion in the hallway, with a rush

of doctors and nurses. Time passed, and they came to find me. With tears in their eyes, they told me, "Your wife has died." At that moment, I was devastated. The pressures of this life became an overwhelming load that I could not bear. I fell to my knees and begged God to bring her back. I told him that if he would bring her back, I would buy a Bible and read it and search to find out who he was.

The doctors came back in and told me they were able to revive her! The next day, I went out and bought a Bible and read Matthew 7:7, "Ask and it will be given to you. Seek and you shall find. Knock and the door will be opened to you."

Despite all my cries, my tears, and my petitions, my wife died six months later, and I was left with a three-year-old and a newborn baby.

Why did this happen? What was I to do? What was the whole purpose of life? I kept thinking about how I was a good person, loved people, and always did my best at anything I did, yet here I was, lost with overwhelming, unanswered questions.

I continued screaming out these questions to God, "Why?" "Why did this happen?" "Why her?" "Why did these children lose their mother?" "Why me?"

The screams that I cried out were from the pain that was deep within my heart. These answers, I decided, I would never find on the face of the earth. So I struggled and pursued and had questions which multiplied into more questions. God was quick to hear and answer my pursuit to know him. He met me where I was at. In just under two years after the death of my wife, I became a follower and disciple of Jesus. I was not living like the men in the Bible who followed the call of Jesus. I thought I was a Christian, but I had never really seen what it meant to walk with and have a daily relationship with Jesus, much less to have a purpose and direction for my life. However, even then, no one had the answers to my questions. None of the men who studied the Bible with me could help me understand why my wife had to die. None of the ministers could give me answers. I continued to ask the question "Why God?" Then, one day, I turned the pages of my Bible to Romans 9:14–23. As I read the passage, remaining silent and listening, I heard God so clearly say to me, "Who are you, Rick, to talk back to me?" and "It will not depend on your efforts anymore." "It will not depend on your will or desire anymore, for I will have mercy on who I want and I will harden and I will destroy who I want." "Stand down, Rick, and fear me, for I am God."

This was a huge turning point in my relationship with God. I decided to stop searching for questions and answers that I would not find in this lifetime, on this earth. God already knows my first question when I meet him in eternity will be, "Why?" "How come?" "I don't understand!" It is a question that only my father in heaven can answer. A question from a son.

When Jesus walked in the garden of Gethsemane, he found himself overwhelmed with sorrow and looked to God for strength to continue. As he pursued God, he overcame fear and found great joy. He trusted in the sovereignty of his Father.

The first-century disciples walked with Jesus yet were filled with wonder and fear at times because they had so many questions about God, Jesus, and life that they struggled with. They learned, from Jesus, to trust the sovereignty of God.

God knows the truth, and because of that, I find peace. I find strength. I cannot find confidence. And yet one day, I will. For me, it is a special relationship that I have with God. It is something that no man or woman can ever understand. I'm chosen to carry a burden, yet I find such joy in being trustworthy and responsible with it. I learned to trust the sovereignty of God.

My brothers and sisters, if we follow his example and do the same day by day, year after year, we will find the joy that will fill the darkest recesses of our hearts. Because God is sovereign, Jesus said we will be more than conquerors! Literally, we will overcome the fear of death. Those of you who have experienced this and understand the victory that God has given you, you know the joy! And those of you that have not found this place of fear and joy yet, continue to pursue God. God is sovereign!

For further study:

Job 1:20
Proverbs 16:25, 20:5,30
Matthew 7:7–8

Rick Norris
El Cajon, CA

NOTES

Title
I Have Seen God's *Support*

Definition: preventing from falling, sinking, etc.; the act of assisting
or strengthening morally
Theme scripture: Deuteronomy 33:27

> The eternal God is your refuge, and underneath
> are the everlasting arms.

What comes to mind when you think of support? Is the first picture in your mind that of God's arms? All around us, everything in life and on this earth work in incredible concert. My mind is blown away every time I think at the miracle of the earth revolving around the sun at just the right speed and distance. That support and provision can only come from our SUPPORTIVE God and Father. Everything around us is perfectly supported to turn our eyes and heart to him.

In the garden of Eden, God supported and provided everything that Adam and Eve would need to sustain their lives, and all of it was provided before Adam and Eve existed. God has always supported his children in good times and bad. The support may not have always come in the way expected or desired, but it was and is always there. I think of those times of support during tough times or tragedies. God supported the children of Israel as they finally were released from bondage, not with just the clothes on their backs, but with articles of silver and gold and clothing from the Egyptians. The Israelites plundered those who had kept them in bondage through the provision of God (Exodus 13). How many different ways did God support Joseph during his life, from his brothers' hatred to being able to provide and support his family during the famine? (Genesis 37–45). What must the five thousand men have thought when they expected to eat, but all that was available were five small barley loaves and two small fish? The disciples doubted where the provision would come from; however, Jesus and God knew that the physical provision of multiplied food would open the hearts of all in attendance to see God's spiritual provision. (John 6). Job feels and knows the depths and strength of God's arms as he faced significant losses of family members and things, only to be provided for beyond what he could imagine. It seems that God's supportive arms are greater during times of great challenges and loss.

In 1988, our second daughter, Christy, was born. We had great hopes of our girls growing strong and healthy. Something happened when she was nearing her first birthday. We still to this day don't know what it was, but it left her with the diagnosis of autism. God's support at that time was through some of our friends and through the various agencies that diagnosed her and provided a treatment plan. By the time we had become disciples in 1993, Christy was at a great school, and other disciples were supporting us through babysitting our special-needs child, along with our now two other children. July 1997 would be a time of loss and great pain as we lost Christy to a pool accident. God's arms, though not entirely physically present, were present through the arms of those who supported us through this time. Psalm 46:1 was the scripture I clung to as I truly needed the refuge of God and all of his support to deal with losing a child, and continuing to be a wife and mother to my other children. I didn't know that his support through this time would be what we would need for the next challenge. July 1998, our youngest, Kelly, was diagnosed with multiple sclerosis. This is extremely rare in children, and at that time, she was the only pediatric case in San Diego. God's arms of support were not only evident in all the times we were in and out of the hospital, but I caught a glimpse of how, through Christy's death, we were supported. It would have been incredibly difficult to split my time between a special-needs child at home and one in the hospital. God provided what we needed to be there fully for Kelly. I won't forget the many that would visit us in the hospital intensive care unit to sit and pray with us. I won't forget how God provided a disciple nurse at that very hospital, who would always take Kelly as his patient for his shift. Mike would even have quiet times with Kelly or just simply read to her. What great and awesome provision our God has for us! An older woman, Barb, showed me the passage in Deuteronomy, and she helped me to see all the instances of God' supportive arms, even in the darkness of the challenges. In January 2001, Kelly lost her battle with that devastating disease. God's arms were even more evident as I understood his gift of provision and support for us. We were and continue to be surrounded by the family of God that hugs us, lifts us up, or extends the arms of comfort when needed. How incredible to feel God's arms in that way.

As we allowed the comfort and strength of God's arms through others to lift us out of the depths, I could see how God didn't allow us to sink. He strengthened us spiritually so that we could continue to serve him. I see his gift as a new perspective of families with special-needs children or those who've suffered loss. It's so special to really be able to say to someone, "I know what you're going through, and this is how I was supported by God to get to this place."

For further study:

Isaiah 41:9–10
Psalm 46
1 Peter 5:10

Karen Nicholson
San Diego, CA

NOTES

Title

I Have Seen God's *Thoughfulness*

Definition: having or showing heed for the well-being or happiness
    of others and a propensity for anticipating their needs or wishes
Theme scripture: Psalms 8:4

> What are mere mortals that you should think
> about them, human beings that you should care
> for them?

Our God is a THOUGHTFUL God. When you read the Bible,
you see how God went to great lengths to give and to make himself
known. He thought through each and every decision and situation
so that we could have the opportunity to draw close to him. That
amazes me about him.

In the Old Testament, as he creates everything in the beginning,
I am amazed at how every moment is so specific. When I think about
Moses going before Pharaoh, God gave him Aaron by his side to go
with him. With Gideon, we watch God planning the details of his
life and seeing in him what he knows he can be, even when he can't
see it himself. Joseph, from when he was a child, was guided by God
through every trial to eventually save a nation. He orchestrates each
and every moment to help his people stand together and bring glory
to him. He cares about each individual deeply. As he works, he constantly assures us that he is with us and that he will never leave us.
When he sewed loyalty into Ruth's heart, he made sure Boaz would
be there to care for her. Over and over again throughout the scriptures, God's thoughtfulness is evident.

And it is evident in my life as well, because God thinks about me and cares for me.

It was Thanksgiving morning, 1992. Most people that I knew were cooking turkeys, making way too many side dishes, and having family over for the day. Even the people on television seemed to be celebrating.

I was mourning. I was afraid. I was unsure. My husband, Ted, had died only thirty hours earlier. I had two small children and had no idea where my life was headed.

However, God knew. I got up early to have some time with God before the kids got up. In tears as I came before God, I felt so loved. I realized that only as a Christian could I have just gone through the hardest time of my life and still had so much to be grateful for! My whole quiet time that morning was on a typical Thanksgiving morning subject, but with a different heart and spirit than I had ever had. I truly felt humbled in God's presence at seeing all the ways that God had been so thoughtful throughout Ted's illness.

Two years before Ted died, our family had moved to a smaller church in South Carolina. God was meeting a need we didn't know we had by allowing us to be in a smaller group of Christians that truly understood Southern hospitality. We had just lost our jobs a week before my husband was diagnosed. At the time, it forced me to search the Bible for subjects like faithfulness, contentment, trust, etc. Little did I know that in that moment, it was for a job; a week later, it would be the same lessons but for my husband's life and our future. I had a baby just two weeks after his diagnosis. Again, I saw that God always brings joy in the midst of our storms. He is so thoughtful. We had so many close friends and family that made themselves available to serve and help us in every way. God is a relational God, and he is constantly trying to help us see how much we need each other. God provided a way for us to go back to NYC to be in one of the best cancer hospitals in the world. In providing that, he also allowed us to be with many of our spiritually strong friends there.

One last way that God was so thoughtful was with the gift of time. We had time to talk through the "what-ifs." We shed many tears taking the time to have difficult talks that we knew we needed to have. Ted got to write letters to his best friends. The night before he died was the only full night I spent in the hospital in NYC with him. I believe God was thoughtful in that and gave us that last night.

Just like the men and women I had read about for years in the Bible, God was thinking about me and caring for me. He was planning for me and loving me. Look for how God has been thoughtful to you in your life, even in the most difficult times. You will be amazed.

Scriptures for study:

Psalm 8:3–4
1 Samuel 12:24
Psalm 77

Kathi Norris
El Cajon, CA

NOTES

CPSIA information can be obtained
at www.ICGtesting.com
Printed in the USA
BVHW071410190421
605294BV00003B/560